*For Judy, Brian, Kira,
David & Micol
and all the children and
families of Temple Emanu-El
S.Z.*

The publication of this prayerbook is made
possible through the generosity of
Rhea Fay Fruhman,
the late Leo Fruhman,
and their son Leonard Fruhman

THE FAMILY PRAYERBOOK

The Fall Holy Days

SHELDON ZIMMERMAN

Illustrations by

ELEANOR SCHICK

ROSEL BOOKS

Dallas, Texas

© Copyright 1989 by Temple Emanu-El of Dallas, Texas

All rights reserved.

*Our gratitude to Seymour Rossel for his thoughtful, spiritual,
and creative editing and guidance;
and to Susan Salom for her caring help.*

*ISBN 0-940646-59-5
Typesetting and Design by R.C.C.*

Distributed by
BEHRMAN HOUSE, INC.
235 Watchung Avenue
West Orange, NJ 07052

CONTENTS

Rosh Hashanah	6
Yom Kippur	16
Sukkot	26
Simhat Torah	34
Closing Prayers	43

ROSH HASHANAH

[ROSH HASHANAH SONG]

The New Year is a time of beginnings. Begin now by turning to the persons sitting to the left of you and to the right of you, in front of you and behind you. Say, *"Shana tovah umetukah!* May you have a good and sweet year!"

ALL

שָׁנָה טוֹבָה וּמְתוּקָה!

May you have a good and sweet year!

"How good it is and how pleasant when people come together in friendship."

הִנֵּה מַה־טּוֹב וּמַה־נָּעִים, שֶׁבֶת אַחִים גַּם־יָחַד.

Hinei mah tov umana-im, shevet achim gam yachad.

Beginnings are times of new hope.
    Beginning a new year or starting a new class,
Joining a new club, learning a new sport, entering a new school,
    As we enter upon the new, we leave the past behind.
We look forward, mixing emotions with visions.
    Dreams and hopes light our path into the future.

Rosh Hashanah is our holiday of visions, hopes, and dreams.
    On this new year, we pray for a fresh beginning —
On this new year, we pray for joy and friendship, love and peace.
    On this new year, we pray for health and blessing.
On this new year, we pray for wisdom, humility, and kindness.
    On this new year, we pray for love in our lives, and love in all lives.
On this new year, we pray for God's Presence as we renew our study of Torah.
    On this new year, we pray for peace for our family; peace for all families.
On this new year, we give thanks to God for allowing us to reach this day:

בָּרוּךְ אַתָּה, יְיָ אֱלֹהֵינוּ, מֶלֶךְ הָעוֹלָם,
שֶׁהֶחֱיָנוּ וְקִיְּמָנוּ וְהִגִּיעָנוּ לַזְּמַן הַזֶּה.

Baruch atah, Adonai — **We praise You,** *Adonai,*
**for giving us life, health, and strength;
for bringing us to this New Year.** *Amen.*

ALL RISE

בָּרְכוּ אֶת יְיָ הַמְבֹרָךְ.
Let us praise God.

בָּרוּךְ יְיָ הַמְבֹרָךְ לְעוֹלָם וָעֶד.
We praise God now and forever.

Rosh Hashanah is the birthday of the world. On this day, our sages say, God created light, and began creating the entire universe. For light and for darkness; for the sun by day, the moon and stars by night; for earth, wind, and fire, we give thanks to God for this singular work we call Creation.

FOR GOD'S CREATION

Baruch atah Adonai — We Praise You, *Adonai,*
   For the amazing universe of which we are a part.
For the glory of daybreak; for the quietude of nightfall;
   For the order of nature, season following season.

בָּרוּךְ אַתָּה, יְיָ, יוֹצֵר הַמְּאוֹרוֹת.

**We praise You, O God, for the order of night and day,
for the brightness of the sun and for the wonder of our lives.**

[ROSH HASHANAH SONG]

FOR THE GIFT OF TORAH

With a great love You love us, O God,
  Your Torah is a light for our path, a guide for our lives.
May our eyes grow bright in the study of Your Torah.
  May our hearts and actions be faithful to Your *mitzvot*.
May we learn to love You as You love us.
  We thank You O God, for giving us the Torah, Your most precious gift.
We thank You, O God, for Your Torah, Your great gift of love.

THE SHEMA

שְׁמַע יִשְׂרָאֵל: יְיָ אֱלֹהֵינוּ, יְיָ אֶחָד.

Hear, O Israel: The Lord is our God, the Lord is One.

בָּרוּךְ שֵׁם כְּבוֹד מַלְכוּתוֹ לְעוֹלָם וָעֶד.

Praised be God whose Rule is forever.

וְאָהַבְתָּ אֵת יְיָ אֱלֹהֶיךָ בְּכָל־לְבָבְךָ וּבְכָל־נַפְשְׁךָ וּבְכָל־מְאֹדֶךָ. וְהָיוּ הַדְּבָרִים הָאֵלֶּה, אֲשֶׁר אָנֹכִי מְצַוְּךָ הַיּוֹם, עַל־לְבָבֶךָ. וְשִׁנַּנְתָּם לְבָנֶיךָ, וְדִבַּרְתָּ בָּם בְּשִׁבְתְּךָ בְּבֵיתֶךָ, וּבְלֶכְתְּךָ בַדֶּרֶךְ וּבְשָׁכְבְּךָ וּבְקוּמֶךָ.

וּקְשַׁרְתָּם לְאוֹת עַל־יָדֶךָ, וְהָיוּ לְטֹטָפֹת בֵּין עֵינֶיךָ. וּכְתַבְתָּם עַל־מְזֻזוֹת בֵּיתֶךָ, וּבִשְׁעָרֶיךָ.

לְמַעַן תִּזְכְּרוּ וַעֲשִׂיתֶם אֶת־כָּל־מִצְוֹתָי. וִהְיִיתֶם קְדֹשִׁים לֵאלֹהֵיכֶם. אֲנִי יְיָ אֱלֹהֵיכֶם, אֲשֶׁר הוֹצֵאתִי אֶתְכֶם מֵאֶרֶץ מִצְרַיִם לִהְיוֹת לָכֶם לֵאלֹהִים. אֲנִי יְיָ אֱלֹהֵיכֶם.

You shall love *Adonai* your God
  With all your strength and mind.
These words which I command you today —
  Keep them close to your heart.

Teach them to your children,
> **Say them over and again.**

In the evening and in the morning,
> **Wherever you may be,**

When you speak, when you are silent,
> **Keep them close, very close.**

Copy these words;
> **Set them before you.**

On the doorposts of your homes,
> **And on your gates.**

So that you will remember your God
> **And do all of God's commandments,**

Today and every day of your life.

FOR THE PROMISE OF REDEMPTION

בָּרוּךְ אַתָּה, יְיָ, גָּאַל יִשְׂרָאֵל.

We remember a time long before we were born,
> **Our people left the Holy Land to settle in the land of Egypt.**

Then Pharaoh and his people enslaved us —
> **They forced us to work as slaves and robbed us of our freedom.**

With an outstretched arm and a mighty hand, God brought us out of Egypt.
> **God taught us to hate slavery and love freedom.**

To act in the Image of God, we must do what God has done.
> **We must set the captive free; we must rescue the slave from slavery.**

Baruch atah, Adonai, Ga-al Yisrael.
> **We praise You, *Adonai* — Redeemer of Israel.**

TEFILLAH

We praise You, *Adonai*, our God, God of our Fathers and Mothers, God of all generations. Your ways are loving as you heal the sick and free the captive, as you send help to the falling and comfort all who suffer pain.

We praise You, O God,
> **For the holiness of the world,**

For the holiness of Rosh Hashanah,
> **For the holiness of life.**

We praise You, O God,
> **Source of holiness.**

Baruch atah, Adonai, hamelech hakadosh.

לְשָׁנָה טוֹבָה תִּכָּתֵבוּ!

L'shanah tovah tikatevu!
Happy New Year to you!

KEDUSHAT HAYOM – THE HOLINESS OF THIS DAY

On Rosh Hashanah we celebrate a beginning, the birthday of the world and the start of a new year. And on Rosh Hashanah we celebrate an ending, too. For all its good and all its bad, last year is behind us now. Yet, on our High Holy Days we take one last long look behind, especially to see how we might have done just a little better, the things that we would really like to change.

We thank You, God, for the year that has passed.
> **We tried to do our best, but our best was not always good enough.**

At times we aimed too high and missed our aim, or forgot ourselves and did things we knew we should not do.
> **We made mistakes, and we are sorry for the mistakes we made.**

A new year starts with this High Holy Day season.
> **Help us, O God, to do the best we can with the gifts You have given us.**

Help us to use our strengths and our talents to make the world a better place for all.

בָּרוּךְ אַתָּה, יְיָ, מֶלֶךְ עַל כֹּל הָאָרֶץ.
מְקַדֵּשׁ יִשְׂרָאֵל [הַשַּׁבָּת] וְיוֹם הַזִּכָּרוֹן.

We praise You, Adonai, Ruler of the entire universe,
Who makes us holy, and Who makes this day
of remembering holy, too. *Amen.*

WORSHIP, THANKSGIVING, AND PEACE

Thank you, God, for family and friends.

Thank You, God, for all the wonderful moments and people in my life.

Thank You, God, for the opportunity to worship and pray in this beautiful place.

Thank You, God, for filling our world with beauty.

Now help us work for *Shalom* — Your blessing and gift of peace.

We know that even when it feels like *Shalom* is a distant dream,

You promised that peace can be real, if only we strive for it and seek it out.

If we care for others just as we should care for ourselves,

Then *Shalom* will follow — for you, for me, for our people in Israel, for all people wherever they may be.

עֹשֶׂה שָׁלוֹם בִּמְרוֹמָיו. הוּא יַעֲשֶׂה שָׁלוֹם
עָלֵינוּ וְעַל־כָּל־יִשְׂרָאֵל. וְאִמְרוּ: אָמֵן.

Oseh shalom bim'romav, hu ya-a-seh shalom aleinu
V'al kol Yisrael, v'imru, amen. Ya-aseh shalom.

We close our eyes and pray quietly, saying words without sound.

SILENT PRAYER

May the words of my mouth echo God's words,
May the thoughts in my heart ever be thoughts of God. *Amen.*

SHOFAR SERVICE

Thousands of years ago our ancestors called Rosh Hashanah, *"yom zichron teruah"* — the day recalling the *shofar*'s sound.

The *shofar*'s call is an alarm. It wakes us up — a new year has come! It reminds us of the time — another year has ended! There is so much we wanted to do and, instead, it seems we did so little. There are so many things we wanted to say — to parents, grandparents, and friends — and, instead, it seems we forgot to say them. Time is fleet, flying past us on gossamer wings. The *shofar* cries out, "Do the things you want to do now. Say the words you want to say now. Be what you want to be now. If not now, when?"

בָּרוּךְ אַתָּה, יְיָ אֱלֹהֵינוּ, מֶלֶךְ הָעוֹלָם, אֲשֶׁר קִדְּשָׁנוּ בְּמִצְוֹתָיו, וְצִוָּנוּ לִשְׁמֹעַ קוֹל שׁוֹפָר.

We praise You *Adonai*, our God, Ruler of the universe, for making us holy through Your *mitzvot*, and commanding us to hear the voice of the *shofar*.

בָּרוּךְ אַתָּה, יְיָ אֱלֹהֵינוּ, מֶלֶךְ הָעוֹלָם, שֶׁהֶחֱיָנוּ וְקִיְּמָנוּ וְהִגִּיעָנוּ לַזְּמַן הַזֶּה.

We praise You *Adonai*, our God, Ruler of the universe, for giving us life, health, and strength; for bringing us to this day so that we could hear the *shofar*'s sound. *Amen*.

THE SHOFAR IS SOUNDED

תְּקִיעָה.
The shofar says, "Awaken, O My people Israel."

שְׁבָרִים.
The shofar says, "Remember who you are, O Israel!"

תְּרוּעָה.
The shofar says, "You are Israel! You must never lose hope!"

תְּקִיעָה.
"When you are My people Israel, you do not stand alone!"

תְּקִיעָה.
The shofar says, "Be Jews, O My people Israel!"

שְׁבָרִים.
"The Jewish new year is before you!"

תְּרוּעָה.
"Find new ways of doing what is right; dream new dreams!"

תְּקִיעָה.
"Reach out and embrace both family and friends!"

תְּקִיעָה.
"Do what is just, what is true, and what is kind!"

שְׁבָרִים.
"Walk in My paths, O My people Israel!"

תְּרוּעָה.
"Choose life that you and your people may live!"

תְּקִיעָה גְדוֹלָה.
"Choose God so that God will choose you and yours in this New Year!"

SERMON

CLOSING PRAYERS: PAGE 43

ADON OLAM

אֲדוֹן עוֹלָם, אֲשֶׁר מָלַךְ, בְּטֶרֶם כָּל־יְצִיר נִבְרָא.
לְעֵת נַעֲשָׂה בְחֶפְצוֹ כֹּל, אֲזַי מֶלֶךְ שְׁמוֹ נִקְרָא.

וְאַחֲרֵי כִּכְלוֹת הַכֹּל, לְבַדּוֹ יִמְלוֹךְ נוֹרָא.
וְהוּא הָיָה, וְהוּא הֹוֶה, וְהוּא יִהְיֶה בְּתִפְאָרָה.

וְהוּא אֶחָד. וְאֵין שֵׁנִי לְהַמְשִׁיל לוֹ. לְהַחְבִּרָה.
בְּלִי רֵאשִׁית. בְּלִי תַכְלִית. וְלוֹ הָעֹז וְהַמִּשְׂרָה.

וְהוּא אֵלִי. וְחַי גּוֹאֲלִי. וְצוּר חֶבְלִי בְּעֵת צָרָה.
וְהוּא נִסִּי וּמָנוֹס לִי. מְנָת כּוֹסִי בְּיוֹם אֶקְרָא.

בְּיָדוֹ אַפְקִיד רוּחִי בְּעֵת אִישַׁן וְאָעִירָה.
וְעִם־רוּחִי גְוִיָּתִי: יְיָ לִי, וְלֹא אִירָא.

YOM KIPPUR

מַה טֹּבוּ אֹהָלֶיךָ, יַעֲקֹב, מִשְׁכְּנֹתֶיךָ, יִשְׂרָאֵל!
Mah tovu ohalechah, Ya-akov, mish'k'notechah, Yisrael!

Today is Yom Kippur. At a Shabbat service, we would say, "*Shabbat shalom.*" On any other holiday, we might say, "*Hag samei'ach,*" or "Happy Holiday." But not on Yom Kippur. On Shabbat and other holidays, we spend some time at Temple. At home, we sit around our tables and sing songs, say the *kiddush* to bless the wine, and eat special foods. But not on Yom Kippur. On Yom Kippur, we greet each other with the special phrase, "*Gemar hatimah tovah,*" "May your name be sealed in the Book of Life for the year to come." On Yom Kippur, most Jews—those Bar and Bat Mitzvah age, and older—try not to eat any food the whole day. We call this act of not eating, "fasting." Yom Kippur is a day of fasting.

Yom Kippur is a day for looking deeply at ourselves.
   Yom Kippur is a quiet day; we come to Temple to think and pray.
Our thoughts turn to God and the special part God plays in our lives.
   Our thoughts turn inward to ask, "What kind of person have I been?"
"How have I acted in this year that has passed?"
   Did we always do the right thing? Did we always do our best?
We look back to ask, Could we have done better if we tried a little harder?
   Did we blame others when we should rightly have blamed ourselves?
Yom Kippur is a time for saying, "I'm sorry," and really meaning it.
   On Yom Kippur we remember what we did to help us learn to do better.

KOL NIDREI

An old and wise prayer is recited by Jews everywhere each Yom Kippur evening. Its name is *Kol Nidrei*. Its music is haunting and ancient. Now listen to its sound:

כָּל־נִדְרֵי וֶאֱסָרֵי וַחֲרָמֵי וְקוֹנָמֵי וְכִנּוּיֵי וְקִנּוּסֵי...

Do not hold us to our promises to You, O God, if we can not keep them. For we mean well when we make promises, but You know we are only human, and human beings sometimes forget, sometimes promise things more than they can keep, and often make mistakes.

The *Kol Nidrei* prayer calls us together as Jews, reminding us of who we are. So, let us rise and praise God together.

ALL RISE

בָּרְכוּ אֶת יְיָ הַמְבֹרָךְ.

Let us praise God.

בָּרוּךְ יְיָ הַמְבֹרָךְ לְעוֹלָם וָעֶד.

We praise God now and forever.

All year long we have been making choices. We had to choose who would be our friends and who would not. We had to choose what to eat, what television program to watch, what to say, and what to do. We made many choices, but not every choice was a good one.

At times, we said the wrong thing to parents, brothers, sisters, or friends. We did not mean for our words to hurt them, but they were hurt, nonetheless. At times, we even spoke words in anger. Perhaps we wanted to take those words back. But, once we had spoken them, they could not be changed.

On Yom Kippur we say "*selihah*," "I am sorry." It seems easier to say, "I am sorry," when others are saying it, too. We all must learn to say "*selihah*" — "I am sorry for whatever I did that hurt you." For a few moments, think to yourself: "What did I do that might have hurt someone?"

CHOIR

וְעַל כֻּלָּם, אֱלוֹהַּ סְלִיחוֹת,
סְלַח לָנוּ, מְחַל לָנוּ, כַּפֶּר־לָנוּ!

V'al kulam, eloha selihot,
Selah lanu, mehal lanu, ka-peir lanu!

Turn to your parents, grandparents, friends, brothers, sisters — whoever is sitting beside you. Give that person a hug. Now, repeat after me — looking at each other, saying to each other:

Selihah.
   Selihah.
I am sorry.
   I am sorry.
For anything I might have said that hurt you, I am sorry.
   For anything I might have said that hurt you, I am sorry.
For anything I might have done that hurt you, I am sorry.
   For anything I might have done that hurt you, I am sorry.
For anything I forgot to do that I should have done, I am sorry.
   For anything I forgot to do that I should have done, I am sorry.
Selihah — Please forgive me.
   Selihah — **Please forgive me.**

From deep inside, from our heart of hearts, with all the love we have to offer, let us say to one another:

Salahti — I forgive you.
   Salahti — **I forgive you.**

And one more time. Say it to one another and mean it:

Salahti — I forgive you.
   Salahti — **I forgive you.**

Hug one another again. Your hug has new meaning now. Make it a hug of pure lovingkindness. Now that other people have forgiven us, we can turn to God. We all rise to recite the prayer which—more than any other—tells us about God, about our love for God, and about God's love for us.

שְׁמַע יִשְׂרָאֵל: יְיָ אֱלֹהֵינוּ, יְיָ אֶחָד.

Hear, O Israel: The Lord is our God, the Lord is One.

בָּרוּךְ שֵׁם כְּבוֹד מַלְכוּתוֹ לְעוֹלָם וָעֶד.

Praised be God whose Rule is forever.

וְאָהַבְתָּ אֵת יְיָ אֱלֹהֶיךָ בְּכָל־לְבָבְךָ וּבְכָל־נַפְשְׁךָ וּבְכָל־מְאֹדֶךָ. וְהָיוּ הַדְּבָרִים הָאֵלֶּה, אֲשֶׁר אָנֹכִי מְצַוְּךָ הַיּוֹם, עַל־לְבָבֶךָ. וְשִׁנַּנְתָּם לְבָנֶיךָ, וְדִבַּרְתָּ בָּם בְּשִׁבְתְּךָ בְּבֵיתֶךָ, וּבְלֶכְתְּךָ בַדֶּרֶךְ וּבְשָׁכְבְּךָ וּבְקוּמֶךָ.

וּקְשַׁרְתָּם לְאוֹת עַל־יָדֶךָ, וְהָיוּ לְטֹטָפֹת בֵּין עֵינֶיךָ. וּכְתַבְתָּם עַל־מְזֻזוֹת בֵּיתֶךָ, וּבִשְׁעָרֶיךָ.

לְמַעַן תִּזְכְּרוּ וַעֲשִׂיתֶם אֶת־כָּל־מִצְוֹתָי, וִהְיִיתֶם קְדֹשִׁים לֵאלֹהֵיכֶם. אֲנִי יְיָ אֱלֹהֵיכֶם, אֲשֶׁר הוֹצֵאתִי אֶתְכֶם מֵאֶרֶץ מִצְרַיִם לִהְיוֹת לָכֶם לֵאלֹהִים. אֲנִי יְיָ אֱלֹהֵיכֶם.

You shall love *Adonai* your God
   With all your strength and mind.
These words which I command you today—
   Keep them close to your heart.
Teach them to your children,
   Say them over and again.
In the evening and in the morning,
   Wherever you may be,
When you speak, when you are silent,
   Keep them close, very close.

Copy these words;
>   **Set them before you.**

On the doorposts of your homes,
>   **And on your gates.**

So that you will remember your God
>   **And do all of God's commandments,**

Today and every day of your life.

With thoughts of God uppermost in our minds, we are ready to ask for God's forgiveness. There were times when we did not tell the truth — we were not honest. There were times when we failed to respect our religion or our Temple. There were times when we used God's name to make promises that we did not keep. For these things, for all the things we have done wrong, we ask God's forgiveness. We say:

Al heit shehatanu —
>   *Al heit shehatanu —*

For the sins which we committed, we are sorry.
>   *Al heit shehatanu.*

For not always trying to be the best we could be,
>   *Al heit shehatanu.*

For times when we forgot to honor our parents, grandparents, and teachers,
>   *Al heit shehatanu.*

For times we acted badly even when no one was watching,
>   *Al heit shehatanu.*

For times we were unfair to others; for times we hurt others without their knowing,
>   *Al heit shehatanu.*

For times we blamed others for things we had done,
>   *Al heit shehatanu.*

V'al culam, eloha selihot —
>   **For all of these, O God of forgiveness and love —**

Selah lanu,
>   **Forgive us,**

Mehal lanu,
> **Pardon us,**

Ca-peir lanu.
> **Bring us close to You on this Yom Kippur — this Day of Atonement.**

> **O God of forgiveness and love, on this Yom Kippur help us change our ways. Give us always the courage and strength to do what is right and what is pleasing in Your sight. Be with us when we do well. But, even more, in our moments of weakness — at times when we miss the mark — show us Your love and patience. Grant us always the wisdom to change and the strength to try.**

> בָּרוּךְ אַתָּה, יְיָ, מְקוֹר מְחִילָה וְרַחֲמִים.
> **We praise You, O God, source of forgiveness and kindness.**

We close our eyes and pray quietly, saying the words without sound. We think of ways we could try harder and do better next year.

SILENT PRAYER

> **May the words of my mouth echo God's words,**
> **May the thoughts in my heart ever be thoughts of God.** *Amen.*

TORAH SERVICE

V'zot haTorah — This is the Torah. In this scroll we find the stories of our people's beginnings. We read about Abraham, Rebecca, Moses, Aaron, and Miriam. Studying Torah, we learn the highest values of our faith. Listening to its words, we feel the Presence of God who is the source of love and goodness.

ALL RISE

AVINU MALKEINU

אָבִינוּ מַלְכֵּנוּ, חָנֵּנוּ וַעֲנֵנוּ, כִּי אֵין בָּנוּ מַעֲשִׂים.
עֲשֵׂה עִמָּנוּ צְדָקָה וָחֶסֶד וְהוֹשִׁיעֵנוּ.

Avinu malkeinu, haneinu va'aneinu, ki ein banu ma-aseem,
Aseh imanu, tzedakah va-hesed ve-hoshi-einu.

THE TORAH IS TAKEN FROM THE ARK

שְׁמַע יִשְׂרָאֵל: יְיָ אֱלֹהֵינוּ, יְיָ אֶחָד.

Hear, O Israel: The Lord is our God, the Lord is One.

The Torah reading for Yom Kippur afternoon is taken from the Book of Leviticus, Chapter 19. It tells us how to make ourselves *kedoshim* — "holy people." It speaks of *mitzvot* which help us reach for holiness. When we keep these *mitzvot*, acting them out day by day, we draw near to God, increasing goodness in the world.

THE TORAH IS READ

HAFTARAH

We read from the book of the prophet Isaiah. Isaiah lived thousands of years ago, yet he spoke in words which still ring clear to us today.

Is this the fast that I desire?
A day for people to starve their bodies?
Do you call that a fast,
A day when God is close to you?
No, this is the kind of fast I desire:
Share your bread with the hungry;
Take the poor into your home and give them shelter;
When you see the naked, clothe them.
If you offer your kindness to the hungry,
Feeding those who have nothing to eat —
Then your light will shine in the darkness,
And your sadness shall disappear in the noonday sun.

ALL RISE

We have read from the Torah and studied a lesson from Prophets. It is time to return the Torah to the Ark. Yet Torah study goes on. The doors of the Ark are never locked; the Torah is never chained inside it. We study it here in our Temple. We study it in our school. Night and day we think about its lessons. It is our life and the length of our days.

עֵץ־חַיִּים הִיא לַמַּחֲזִיקִים בָּהּ, וְתֹמְכֶיהָ מְאֻשָּׁר.
דְּרָכֶיהָ דַרְכֵי־נֹעַם, וְכָל־נְתִיבוֹתֶיהָ שָׁלוֹם.

**Eitz hayyim hi — It is a tree of life
To them that hold fast to it,
And all its supporters are happy.**

SERMON

CLOSING PRAYERS: PAGE 43

ALL THE WORLD

All the world shall come to serve You
    And bless Your glorious Name,
And Your righteousness triumphant
    The islands shall proclaim.
And the peoples shall go seeking
    Who knew You not before,
And the ends of earth shall praise You,
    And tell Your greatness o'er.

They shall build for You their altars,
    Their idols overthrown,
And their graven gods shall shame them,
    As they turn to You alone.
They shall worship You at sunrise,
    And feel Your kingdom's might,
And impart their understanding
    To those astray in night.

With the coming of Your kingdom
    The hills shall shout with song.
And the islands laugh exultant
    That they to God belong.
And through all Your congregations
    So loud Your praise shall ring,
That the utmost peoples, hearing,
    Shall hail You crowned King.

SUKKOT

Hag samei'ach! We welcome the holiday of Sukkot. To greet this day, we light candles, praying that this Sukkot will be a joyous time of thanksgiving.

בָּרוּךְ אַתָּה, יְיָ אֱלֹהֵינוּ, מֶלֶךְ הָעוֹלָם, אֲשֶׁר קִדְּשָׁנוּ בְּמִצְוֹתָיו, וְצִוָּנוּ לְהַדְלִיק נֵר שֶׁל [שַׁבָּת וְשֶׁל] יוֹם טוֹב.

Baruch atah, Adonai — **We praise You,** *Adonai* —
whose *mitzvot* **make us holy** —
for the *mitzvah* **of lighting and blessing**
the [Shabbat and] festival candles.

We also greet Sukkot by chanting a blessing over a cup of wine. We call this *kiddush* — "something made holy." Our religion is holy, this day is a holy day, and our lives can be made holy, too. May the sweetness of this wine remind us of the sweetness of life and the joy of being Jewish.

בָּרוּךְ אַתָּה, יְיָ אֱלֹהֵינוּ, מֶלֶךְ הָעוֹלָם, בּוֹרֵא פְּרִי הַגָּפֶן.

Baruch atah, Adonai — **We praise You,** *Adonai* —
Ruler of the universe, Creator of the fruit of the vine.

Sukkot comes from the Hebrew word *sukkah* — a "hut" or "booth." Thousands of years ago, our people were farmers. They lived in *sukkot* when they left their homes to harvest the fruits and vegetables growing in their fields. And they dwelled in *sukkot* until the harvest was complete.

Long before that, there was another time when our ancestors lived in *sukkot*. When Moses led our people out of Egypt, they built small huts that were part tent and part house. These *sukkot* could easily be moved from place to place.

On this festival of Sukkot, we remember how our ancestors lived. We recall the farmers in ancient Israel. We think of our people wandering in the wilderness, without homes that were solid and strong. So we build a *sukkah*. We eat in it and pray in it to remember days of long ago.

IN THE SUKKAH

בָּרוּךְ אַתָּה, יְיָ אֱלֹהֵינוּ, מֶלֶךְ הָעוֹלָם, אֲשֶׁר קִדְּשָׁנוּ בְּמִצְוֹתָיו, וְצִוָּנוּ לֵישֵׁב בַּסֻּכָּה.

Baruch atah, Adonai — **We praise You,** *Adonai* —
whose *mitzvot* **make us holy** —
for the *mitzvah* **of dwelling in the** *sukkah*.

We thank You, O God, for the kindness you showed our ancestors.
   When they worked so hard to plant and harvest their fields,
When they left their homes and lived in *sukkot* in times of harvest,
   With Your help, the harvests were good ones; there was enough to eat.
As we visit the *sukkah*, we think of them. And we recall that earlier time,
   We remember when our people wandered in the wilderness,
With no solid roof above their heads to protect them from rain and wind,
   We thank you for our homes that provide us with comfort.
We thank you for bringing us to this time, as we recite our call to prayer.

בָּרְכוּ אֶת יְיָ הַמְבֹרָךְ.
Let us praise God.

בָּרוּךְ יְיָ הַמְבֹרָךְ לְעוֹלָם וָעֶד.
We praise God now and forever.

Sukkot is our holiday of thanksgiving. We thank God for the food we eat, the blessings we have. We thank God for plentiful rain and good harvests. We thank God for creating the world.

FOR GOD'S CREATION

Thank You for the beauty around us,
   Trees, flowers, and earth.
Thank You for the radiance around us,
   Sun, moon, and stars.

Thank You for the majesty around us.
> **Thank You, God, for the gift of Your creation:**

For parents, grandparents, and friends.
> **Thank You, God.**

For Torah and *mitzvot*,
> **Thank You, God.**

For our congregation and all it teaches us,
> **We give thanks to You, O God.**

בָּרוּךְ אַתָּה, יְיָ, יוֹצֵר הַמְּאוֹרוֹת.

**We praise You, O God, for the order of night and day,
for the brightness of the sun and for the wonder of our lives.**

FOR THE GIFT OF TORAH

With a great love You love us, O God,
> **Your Torah is a light for our path, a guide for our lives.**

May our eyes grow bright in the study of Your Torah.
> **May our hearts and actions be faithful to Your *mitzvot*.**

May we learn to love You as You love us.
> **We thank You O God, for giving us the Torah, Your most precious gift.**

We thank You, O God, for Your Torah, Your great gift of love.

THE SHEMA

שְׁמַע יִשְׂרָאֵל: יְיָ אֱלֹהֵינוּ, יְיָ אֶחָד.

Hear, O Israel: The Lord is our God, the Lord is One.

בָּרוּךְ שֵׁם כְּבוֹד מַלְכוּתוֹ לְעוֹלָם וָעֶד.

Praised be God whose Rule is forever.

וְאָהַבְתָּ אֵת יְיָ אֱלֹהֶיךָ בְּכָל־לְבָבְךָ וּבְכָל־נַפְשְׁךָ וּבְכָל־מְאֹדֶךָ. וְהָיוּ הַדְּבָרִים הָאֵלֶּה. אֲשֶׁר אָנֹכִי מְצַוְּךָ הַיּוֹם. עַל־לְבָבֶךָ. וְשִׁנַּנְתָּם לְבָנֶיךָ. וְדִבַּרְתָּ בָּם בְּשִׁבְתְּךָ בְּבֵיתֶךָ. וּבְלֶכְתְּךָ בַדֶּרֶךְ וּבְשָׁכְבְּךָ וּבְקוּמֶךָ.

וּקְשַׁרְתָּם לְאוֹת עַל־יָדֶךָ. וְהָיוּ לְטֹטָפֹת בֵּין עֵינֶיךָ. וּכְתַבְתָּם עַל־מְזֻזוֹת בֵּיתֶךָ. וּבִשְׁעָרֶיךָ.

לְמַעַן תִּזְכְּרוּ וַעֲשִׂיתֶם אֶת־כָּל־מִצְוֹתָי. וִהְיִיתֶם קְדֹשִׁים לֵאלֹהֵיכֶם. אֲנִי יְיָ אֱלֹהֵיכֶם. אֲשֶׁר הוֹצֵאתִי אֶתְכֶם מֵאֶרֶץ מִצְרַיִם לִהְיוֹת לָכֶם לֵאלֹהִים. אֲנִי יְיָ אֱלֹהֵיכֶם.

You shall love *Adonai* your God
    With all your strength and mind.
These words which I command you today—
    Keep them close to your heart.
Teach them to your children,
    Say them over and again.
In the evening and in the morning,
    Wherever you may be,
When you speak, when you are silent,
    Keep them close, very close.
Copy these words;
    Set them before you.
On the doorposts of your homes,
    And on your gates.
So that you will remember your God
    And do all of God's commandments,
Today and every day of your life.

בָּרוּךְ אַתָּה, יְיָ, גָּאַל יִשְׂרָאֵל.

Baruch atah, Adonai, Ga-al Yisrael.

We praise You, *Adonai* **— for setting our people free.**

For saving us from the hand of Pharaoh in Egypt,

For teaching us that no person should ever be a slave.

We praise You, *Adonai*, Redeemer of Israel.

[A SUKKOT SONG]

TEFILLAH

We praise You, O God,

For the holiness of the world,

For the holiness [of Sabbaths and] of Sukkot,

For the holiness of life.

We praise You, O God,

Source of holiness.

Baruch atah, Adonai, ha-eil hakadosh.

KEDUSHAT HAYOM – THE HOLINESS OF THIS DAY

We decorate the *sukkah* with leaves, fruits, and vegetables — and sometimes, with pictures and designs. These are not gifts that we can buy. These gifts come from hard work and from the natural goodness of the land on which we live. They are the gifts of food, home, life, and love. The *sukkah* teaches us to give thanks — to each other; to our families and friends; to all those who work with their hands and with their backs so that we can eat and enjoy our lives; and, above all, to God, the Source of all.

When the Pilgrims came to this land, they studied the Bible with care. They read, "After the harvest, you shall celebrate the Festival of Sukkot for seven days, you and your whole family, even the stranger, the orphan, and the widow . . . for God will bless all your crops, and everything you do, and you shall have nothing but joy [Deut. 16:13-15]." From Sukkot, they created the American festival of Thanksgiving.

Yet, even in America, we Jews still celebrate Sukkot as our holiday of history. We fill this festive time with sounds, tastes, smells, things to see, and the *lulav* and *etrog* to hold and to touch.

בָּרוּךְ אַתָּה, יְיָ, מְקַדֵּשׁ [הַשַּׁבָּת וְ] יִשְׂרָאֵל וְהַזְּמַנִּים.

Baruch atah, Adonai — **We praise You,** *Adonai,*
Who makes [Shabbat and] Israel and Sukkot holy. *Amen.*

We close our eyes and pray quietly, saying the words without sound.

SILENT PRAYER

May the words of my mouth echo God's words,
May the thoughts in my heart ever be thoughts of God. *Amen.*

LULAV, ETROG, MYRTLE, AND WILLOW

"Know that on the fifteenth day of the seventh month, when you have gathered in the harvest of your land, you shall observe the festival of *Adonai* to last seven days . . . On the first day you shall take the etrog, branches of palm trees, leafy trees [the myrtle], and willows of the brook, and you shall rejoice before *Adonai* your God seven days [Lev. 23:39-40]."

The four species of the *lulav* and *etrog* remind us of God's gifts.
  We hold them tightly to remind us that our world is precious.
The *lulav* is named for the palm branch. It is straight; it does not bend.
  Like the *lulav*, **Jews must ever walk tall and proud.**
The *etrog* is sweetly scented; its color is a wonder to behold.
  Like the *etrog*, **our Jewish way of life is colorful and sweet.**
The leaf of the willow has the shape of human lips.
  The willow reminds us to choose our words with care.
The leaf of the myrtle has the shape of the human eye.
  The myrtle reminds us to watch carefully, to learn from everything and everyone we see.

בָּרוּךְ אַתָּה, יְיָ אֱלֹהֵינוּ, מֶלֶךְ הָעוֹלָם, אֲשֶׁר קִדְּשָׁנוּ בְּמִצְוֹתָיו, וְצִוָּנוּ עַל־נְטִילַת לוּלָב.

Baruch atah, Adonai — **We praise You, *Adonai* —
whose *mitzvot* make us holy —
for the *mitzvah* of holding and shaking
the *lulav* and *etrog*, the myrtle and willow.**

As we shake the lulav in every direction, we learn that God's Presence is everywhere. God is there when we feel most alone. God shares our weeping and our joy, our sorrow and our celebration.

הוֹדוּ לַייָ כִּי טוֹב, כִּי לְעוֹלָם חַסְדּוֹ!

**Praise and thank *Adonai*, for God is good;
God's kindness lasts forever!**

SERMON

CLOSING PRAYERS. PAGE 43

OSEH SHALOM

עֹשֶׂה שָׁלוֹם בִּמְרוֹמָיו, הוּא יַעֲשֶׂה שָׁלוֹם
עָלֵינוּ וְעַל־כָּל־יִשְׂרָאֵל, וְאִמְרוּ: אָמֵן.
יַעֲשֶׂה שָׁלוֹם.

*Oseh shalom bim'romav, hu ya-a-seh shalom aleinu
V'al kol Yisrael, v'imru, amen.
Ya-aseh shalom.*

SIMHAT TORAH

Tonight we welcome the happy holiday of Simhat Torah. On this day we celebrate the end of a year of Torah study and the beginning of a new year of Torah study. We march with the scrolls of the Torah, we parade with flags held high.

זֶה־הַיּוֹם עָשָׂה יְיָ, נָגִילָה וְנִשְׂמְחָה בוֹ.

This is the day *Adonai* has made: Let us rejoice in it!

We also welcome our consecrants, those children whose lifetime of Torah study has just begun. We greet them in our ancient way:

בְּרוּכִים הַבָּאִים בְּשֵׁם יְיָ.

Blessed are all you who come to study Torah.
May you be blessed in God's Name, today and every day.

[PROCESSIONAL OF CONSECRANTS, ACCOMPANIED BY SIMHAT TORAH SONG]

Now we welcome the holiday with the blessing over the candles, praying that this Simhat Torah will be a sweet and pleasnt time for each of us.

בָּרוּךְ אַתָּה, יְיָ אֱלֹהֵינוּ, מֶלֶךְ הָעוֹלָם, אֲשֶׁר קִדְּשָׁנוּ בְּמִצְוֹתָיו, וְצִוָּנוּ לְהַדְלִיק נֵר שֶׁל [שַׁבָּת וְשֶׁל] יוֹם טוֹב.

Baruch atah, Adonai — **We praise You,** *Adonai* —
whose *mitzvot* make us holy —
for the *mitzvah* of lighting and blessing
the [Shabbat and] festival candles.

Next we chant the blessing over a cup of wine. The *kiddush* blessing reminds us that this is a holy day; that, if we try, we can make our lives holy lives. The wine is the taste of life's sweetness; the sweetness we know when our lives have been made holy.

בָּרוּךְ אַתָּה, יְיָ אֱלֹהֵינוּ, מֶלֶךְ הָעוֹלָם, בּוֹרֵא פְּרִי הַגָּפֶן.

Baruch atah, Adonai — **We praise You,** *Adonai* —
Ruler of the universe, Creator of the fruit of the vine.

The name *Simhat Torah* comes from the Hebrew words *simhah* and *Torah*. *Simhah* is joy and rejoicing. *Torah* has many meanings. It is the name we give the to the scrolls we read in the synagogue. It is also the name that we give to all Jewish study—whatever we study that brings us closer to God is *Torah*. In short, *Torah* is the finest single word in Hebrew for Judaism.

Torah is an exquisite gift. We thank God for this most precious possession which God has given to us. We hold the scrolls of *Torah* close to us as we carry them. Because it is so precious, we do not ever let our study of *Torah* come to an end. As we finish reading the last few verses of the *Torah*, we start all over again reading from the beginning. So we show that *Torah* is eternal. It is always with us, helping us to learn and grow no matter how old we may be. In gratitude for this gift, let us rise to recite together the call to prayer.

בָּרְכוּ אֶת יְיָ הַמְבֹרָךְ.

Let us praise God.

בָּרוּךְ יְיָ הַמְבֹרָךְ לְעוֹלָם וָעֶד.

We praise God now and forever.

FOR GOD'S CREATION

Thank You for the beauty around us,
> **Trees, flowers, and earth.**

Thank You for the radiance around us,
> **Sun, moon, and stars.**

Thank You for the majesty around us.
> **Thank You, God, for the gift of Your creation:**

For parents, grandparents, and friends.
> **Thank You, God.**

For Torah and *mitzvot*,
> **Thank You, God.**

For our congregation and all it teaches us,
> **We give thanks to You, O God.**

בָּרוּךְ אַתָּה, יְיָ, הַמַּעֲרִיב עֲרָבִים.

We praise You, O God, Creator of the twilight.

FOR THE GIFT OF TORAH

With a great love You love us, O God,
   Your Torah is a light for our path, a guide for our lives.
May our eyes grow bright in the study of Your Torah.
   May our hearts and actions be faithful to Your *mitzvot*.
May we learn to love You as You love us.
   We thank You O God, for giving us the Torah, Your most precious gift.
We thank You, O God, for Your Torah, Your great gift of love.

THE SHEMA

שְׁמַע יִשְׂרָאֵל: יְיָ אֱלֹהֵינוּ, יְיָ אֶחָד.

Hear, O Israel: The Lord is our God, the Lord is One.

בָּרוּךְ שֵׁם כְּבוֹד מַלְכוּתוֹ לְעוֹלָם וָעֶד.

Praised be God whose Rule is forever.

וְאָהַבְתָּ אֵת יְיָ אֱלֹהֶיךָ בְּכָל־לְבָבְךָ וּבְכָל־נַפְשְׁךָ וּבְכָל־מְאֹדֶךָ. וְהָיוּ הַדְּבָרִים הָאֵלֶּה, אֲשֶׁר אָנֹכִי מְצַוְּךָ הַיּוֹם, עַל־לְבָבֶךָ. וְשִׁנַּנְתָּם לְבָנֶיךָ. וְדִבַּרְתָּ בָּם בְּשִׁבְתְּךָ בְּבֵיתֶךָ. וּבְלֶכְתְּךָ בַדֶּרֶךְ וּבְשָׁכְבְּךָ וּבְקוּמֶךָ.

וּקְשַׁרְתָּם לְאוֹת עַל־יָדֶךָ. וְהָיוּ לְטֹטָפֹת בֵּין עֵינֶיךָ.
וּכְתַבְתָּם עַל־מְזֻזוֹת בֵּיתֶךָ. וּבִשְׁעָרֶיךָ.

לְמַעַן תִּזְכְּרוּ וַעֲשִׂיתֶם אֶת־כָּל־מִצְוֹתָי. וִהְיִיתֶם קְדֹשִׁים לֵאלֹהֵיכֶם. אֲנִי יְיָ אֱלֹהֵיכֶם. אֲשֶׁר הוֹצֵאתִי אֶתְכֶם מֵאֶרֶץ מִצְרַיִם לִהְיוֹת לָכֶם לֵאלֹהִים. אֲנִי יְיָ אֱלֹהֵיכֶם.

You shall love *Adonai* your God
> **With all your strength and mind.**

These words which I command you today—
> **Keep them close to your heart.**

Teach them to your children,
> **Say them over and again.**

In the evening and in the morning,
> **Wherever you may be,**

When you speak, when you are silent,
> **Keep them close, very close.**

Copy these words;
> **Set them before you.**

On the doorposts of your homes,
> **And on your gates.**

So that you will remember your God
> **And do all of God's commandments,**

Today and every day of your life.

TEFILLAH

We praise You, O God,
> **For the holiness of the world,**

For the holiness [of Sabbaths and] of Simhat Torah,
> **For the holiness of life.**

We praise You, O God,
> **Source of holiness.**

Baruch atah, Adonai, ha-eil hakadosh.

SILENT PRAYER

> **May the words of my mouth echo God's words,**
> **May the thoughts in my heart ever be thoughts of God.** *Amen.*

[WE HONOR FAMILIES WHO HAVE BEEN WITH US FOR THREE GENERATIONS]

THE GENERATIONS — MIDOR LEDOR

Thinking back through all the generations of our people who passed the *Torah* to their children, we recall Moses, Aaron, and Miriam; Joshua, Deborah, and Samuel; our kings — Saul, David, and Solomon. We recall the majesty of our ancient Temple in Jerusalem, standing proud above the hills. We still hear the echos of the words of our prophets and our rabbis. We hear the reverberations of commentaries and codes, of the teachings of the *yeshivot* and the stories of the *Hasidim*. Like us, our ancestors were all children, then parents, then grandparents. Like us, they paid honor to the *Torah*, passing it *midor ledor*, "from generation to generation."

FAMILIES OF THREE GENERATIONS RISE

We recall those who built this Temple and others like it.
    We thank them for creating a place for prayer and study.
We thank them for giving us a place of learning and meeting.
    We thank them for giving us a place to learn Hebrew.
We thank them for giving us a place to share our holidays and festivals.
    Here we learn Torah and we teach Torah.
Here we pass Torah from great grandparent to grandparent,
    From grandparent to parent, from parent to child.
Thank You, God, for the Torah and for all the generations who kept it alive.
    We promise to study it, to hold it dear, to teach it to our children.
Midor ledor, from one generation to the next,
    From us to all the generations of our people forever.

ALL ARE SEATED

We at Temple are grateful for our families who have kept the torch of Torah blazing all these years. They symbolize all the generations of our people. We ask the grandparents and parents of the children about to be consecrated to rise now — as we symbolically pass the Torah to a new generation.

CONSECRATION

As we rejoice with the Torah, we ask all the consecrants to join us on the pulpit.

[RABBI BLESSES THE CHILDREN]

The miniature scrolls of Torah you are holding in your hands are replicas of the scrolls in this Holy Ark. Hold them close to your hearts. Let these small scrolls remind you always of the Torah. Someday soon you will be called to this pulpit to take part in the services. Whe you are thirteen years old you will celebrate your Bar or Bat Mitzvah here, reading from one of these Torah scrolls. Let this Temple be a second home for you. Let our Torah always bring you comfort and blessing; and may you always be a comfort and blessing to your parents, to the Jewish people, to God, and to our Temple.

[THE ARK IS OPENED]

Together, let us say and sing the first Jewish prayer you have learned:

שְׁמַע יִשְׂרָאֵל: יְיָ אֱלֹהֵינוּ, יְיָ אֶחָד.

Hear, O Israel: The Lord is our God, the Lord is One.

[HAKAFOT, ACCOMPANIED BY SIMHAT TORAH SONGS]

[THE TORAH IS READ]

As we return the Torah scrolls to the Ark, we bring to an end our fall festivals. A new year has begun. We pray for health, blessing, and *shalom* in this new year.

עֵץ־חַיִּים הִיא לַמַּחֲזִיקִים בָּהּ, וְתֹמְכֶיהָ מְאֻשָּׁר.
דְּרָכֶיהָ דַרְכֵי־נֹעַם, וְכָל־נְתִיבוֹתֶיהָ שָׁלוֹם.

Eitz hayyim hi — **It is a tree of life**
To them that hold fast to it,
And all its supporters are happy.

SERMON

CLOSING PRAYERS: PAGE 43

CLOSING PRAYERS

ADORATION

עָלֵינוּ לְשַׁבֵּחַ לַאֲדוֹן הַכֹּל, לָתֵת גְּדֻלָּה לְיוֹצֵר בְּרֵאשִׁית,
שֶׁלֹּא עָשָׂנוּ כְּגוֹיֵי הָאֲרָצוֹת, וְלֹא שָׂמָנוּ כְּמִשְׁפְּחוֹת הָאֲדָמָה:
שֶׁלֹּא שָׂם חֶלְקֵנוּ כָּהֶם, וְגוֹרָלֵנוּ כְּכָל־הֲמוֹנָם.

Let us adore the everliving God
    And render praise unto *Adonai*
Who spread out the Heavens and established the earth
    Whose glory is revealed in the Heavens above
And whose greatness is manifest throughout the world
    Adonai is our God, there is none else

וַאֲנַחְנוּ כּוֹרְעִים וּמִשְׁתַּחֲוִים וּמוֹדִים
לִפְנֵי מֶלֶךְ מַלְכֵי הַמְּלָכִים, הַקָּדוֹשׁ בָּרוּךְ הוּא.

Va-a-nach-nu Ko-r'im U-mish-ta-cha-vim U-mo-dim
Lif-nei Me-lech Mal-chei Ham-la-chim
Ha-ka-dosh Ba-ruch Hu

We bow the head in reverence
    And worship *Adonai* our God,
The Holy One, *Hakadosh*.

בַּיּוֹם הַהוּא יִהְיֶה יְיָ אֶחָד וּשְׁמוֹ אֶחָד.

Bayom hahu, bayom hahu yihyeh Adonai echad u'shmo echad.

On that day God shall be One,
    And God's name shall be One.

KADDISH

יִתְגַּדַּל וְיִתְקַדַּשׁ שְׁמֵהּ רַבָּא בְּעָלְמָא דִּי־בְרָא כִרְעוּתֵהּ.
וְיַמְלִיךְ מַלְכוּתֵהּ בְּחַיֵּיכוֹן וּבְיוֹמֵיכוֹן וּבְחַיֵּי דְכָל־בֵּית יִשְׂרָאֵל.
בַּעֲגָלָא וּבִזְמַן קָרִיב. וְאִמְרוּ: אָמֵן.
יְהֵא שְׁמֵהּ רַבָּא מְבָרַךְ לְעָלַם וּלְעָלְמֵי עָלְמַיָּא.
יִתְבָּרַךְ וְיִשְׁתַּבַּח. וְיִתְפָּאַר וְיִתְרוֹמַם וְיִתְנַשֵּׂא. וְיִתְהַדָּר וְיִתְעַלֶּה
וְיִתְהַלָּל שְׁמֵהּ דְּקֻדְשָׁא. בְּרִיךְ הוּא. לְעֵלָּא מִן־כָּל־בִּרְכָתָא
וְשִׁירָתָא. תֻּשְׁבְּחָתָא וְנֶחֱמָתָא דַּאֲמִירָן בְּעָלְמָא. וְאִמְרוּ: אָמֵן.
יְהֵא שְׁלָמָא רַבָּא מִן־שְׁמַיָּא וְחַיִּים עָלֵינוּ וְעַל־כָּל־יִשְׂרָאֵל. וְאִמְרוּ: אָמֵן.

Raise high and glorify the name of God
    Throughout the world God chose to create.
May God's kingdom be built
    In your lifetime, during your days,
And in the lifetime of all the House of Israel,
    Soon, and in a time close at hand.
So let us say, Amen.

Let the name of the Holy One, the Blessed,
    Be praised and glorified,
Be exalted, raised up and honored,
    Be magnified and spread.
Though we know God is above all praises,
    Above all songs of praise, and above all blessings,
Above all kind words we speak in our world,
    Even so, we say, Amen.

Let peace pour from the heavens
    With life for us and for all Israel.
So let us say, Amen.

עֹשֶׂה שָׁלוֹם בִּמְרוֹמָיו. הוּא יַעֲשֶׂה שָׁלוֹם
עָלֵינוּ וְעַל־כָּל־יִשְׂרָאֵל. וְאִמְרוּ: אָמֵן.

Creator of peace in the highest places,
    May God create peace for us and for all Israel.
For this, we say, Amen.

BJE/RMC
006808